20 Ways to Convert
More Website Visitors and
Win More Traffic

Jamie Rice

20 Ways to Convert More Website
Visitors and Win More Traffic

First Edition (2020)

Copyright © Jamie Rice (2020)

Contents

Introduction

This book is designed for busy people. The 'to do' list relating to digital marketing can feel overwhelming and constantly changing. This book will provide you with twenty, no nonsense, actionable techniques.

Use this book as you please, there is no need to read it cover to cover; dip into whichever techniques you feel are the most important for your business currently.

Part 1:

Win More Traffic

1.1 Google Business/Google Local Search

Your Google Business listing has the potential to drive traffic and referrals if your company serves local customers and has a physical address. This isn't just for restaurants and pubs, just about every business can benefit from this free tool.

Google Business listings are now often showing ABOVE organic listings in some instances meaning your business can get to the top of page 1 of Google organic search results with considerably less effort compared to doing so by traditional search engine optimisation means.

How does your business get into this position?

Firstly, if you haven't already done so visit www.google.co.uk/business and claim your business listing. To confirm that you are actually who you say you are. Google will send a postcard with a verification pin number to your business address; when you receive this it's time to login to your Google Business account and enter the code.

What next?

There's a number of factors that will dictate if you're shown on the local search results and in what position. What can you do to increase your chances of success:

- Include your opening hours and all points of contact e.g. website link, email address and contact number.

- Include any attributes that your business listing has e.g. disabled parking, wheelchair accessible entrance, public toilet etc.

- Choose which sector you are in and list what services you offer.

- Business summary. This is currently a maximum of 750 characters, fill this with as much information as possible so potential customers can get a feel for your business.

- The Google Business platform now allows users to post updates which last for a period of 7 days. I have managed to gain considerable exposure by taking advantage of these posts.

- Include as many high quality photographs as possible for each of the relevant areas. Google will like to see imagery broken down into sections such as interior pictures, outside shots, products, members of staff, corporate identity and more.

- Get reviews. Don't go touting for reviews or be tempted to ask your friends or family to write some reviews. Provide a great service and when customers tell you how happy they are, ask them to leave a review on your Google Business listing.

This may sound like a lot but the vast majority can be done in one sitting which may only take around an hour. When you think that this one hour of work may bring in hundreds to thousands of visitors to your website over a year it is well worth taking an hour out of your schedule to do this.

Like anything, the more effort you put in, the higher the rewards are likely to be. Consistently post updates on your business listing and add relevant imagery for maximum results.

1.2 Making website tweaks from Google Search Console/Google Webmaster Tools Research

Google Search Console (used to be known as Google Webmaster Tools, which is what many people still refer to it as) can be a very powerful tool when using this trick.

If you don't have it installed on your site already then it's very quick and simple, particularly if you're running on WordPress. Take a minute to watch a step by step YouTube video. In my experience the quickest way has been to install the Tracking Code Manager plugin on WordPress and then entering the snippet of code provided by Google Search Console when registering your site.

There are many, many features in Google Search Console but we're going to focus on just one to gain some quick wins and maximise results. When the code is placed on your site and it's had a few weeks to collect some data it's time to see what your website is ranking for.

How do I do this?

- Login to Google Search Console.
- On the left hand side of the page click 'Search Traffic'.
- Then click 'Search Analytics'.
- Above the graph, ensure both 'clicks' and 'impressions' are ticked to show two graphs.

What's the difference between a click and an impression?

A click as it suggests is someone who has actually clicked on your website on Google organic search results and subsequently visited your website.

An impression is when someone has conducted a Google search and your site has been displayed out of the possible search results.

The amount of impressions your website receives will be a great deal higher than the number of clicks due to there being so many options for search engine users. This next part is where it comes to working smart; when scrolling through the 'Search Analytics' in Google Search Console you're going to see all the weird and wonderful search terms your website has been found for.

What we're going to do here is a very quick win that a lot of people don't take advantage of. Look for search results which are getting a good number of impressions but little or no clicks (a good number of impressions will depend on how popular your website is now, it could range from a few dozen up to tens of thousands but look for your most popular impressions that has minimal clicks). What does this tell you? It tells you that whatever this search term is, has potential to get traffic, you're just not quite there yet for some reason. Here's how to fix it:

1. Go to Google and enter the search term EXACTLY as it shows in Search Analytics.

2. Find where your website is; if it's getting a lot of impressions it's likely to be near the bottom of page 1 or possibly page 2.

3. Click the link to your website when it appears. Whatever this webpage is, this is the one that is ranking and needs further optimisation to start getting clicks and not just impressions.

How can I move this page up the Google rankings?

There are a number of simple strategies which can allow you to do this, they include:

- Add or alter your pages header tags to include the search term you want to rank for.

- This page is clearly doing something well, but it needs an extra boost, so write some additional useful content.

- Add or alter the meta description and page title of this webpage to ensure that the exact search term is included in both.

- Login to Google Analytics and check the 'bounce rate' of the page; a high bounce rate (60%+) can be a ranking factor; if the bounce rate is high, make the page more engaging. This can be done by adding a video, breaking up chunks of text with nice imagery or header tags.

Consistently login to Google Search Console to look for these search analytics opportunities and track how successful your alterations have been by seeing if the search term has started to receive more clicks. The moves won't happen overnight, but if you implement this strategy almost without doubt your site will start to win more traffic in a long term, sustainable way.

1.3 Using Google 'Searches Related To...' in the footer section of Google Searches

It's time to thank Google for another one of their user-friendly features. When entering a Google search, scroll down to the bottom of the page and you will see a number of suggestions with the title 'Suggestions related to [insert what you originally searched for]'. This is absolute dynamite knowledge!

How does this help me?

These suggested searches are high frequency search terms; by employing this strategy you could significantly increase search engine traffic to your website with very little effort. Let's say you ranked top to middle of page 1 for the long tail search term 'Men's watch engraving' some of the searches related to this are (at time of writing):

- Personalised wrist watch
- Watch engraving near me
- Personalised watches for him
- Personalised engraved men's watches

To have success with one long tail keyword will most likely be due to a blog article or strong service page. If you're not sure, run the Google search and click your listing in the search engine results; the page you land on is the one that is seen as most relevant/performing best for that search.

Now what?

You can now make simple additions to this page. I've found the following to work very well:

1. Place a header tag that states exactly what one of the suggested searches said, e.g. 'Personalised Wrist Watch'.

2. Write around 150-250 words of content underneath this header tag that is useful and interesting.

3. Repeat this process for other related search terms. Don't go crazy and add ten new header tags all containing the related search terms. Pick a few that you would like to rank for and are confident you can create interesting or useful content around.

4. Keep an eye on search ranking for these terms by either using a keyword tracking tool such as Moz or by using the free method of running the Google searches manually.

5. Ranking can be achieved a lot faster for these additional keywords. I've seen results in as little as two weeks. If there's been no progress within a month, go in and add more content, or create an infographic, video, checklist or whatever is relevant for the chosen search term.

1.4 How to quickly gain page 1 Google ranking by going after long tail keywords

Gaining page 1 Google ranking for a competitive search term can be difficult as well as requiring a significant amount of time and investment. By comparison gaining ranking for a 'long tail keyword' can be considerably quicker and easier.

What are long tail keywords?

A keyword can be something such as 'men's watch'; a long tail keyword is this initial keyword phrase and something more specific which makes it 'long tail', e.g. 'Men's watch engraving ideas'. I can choose this as an example with confidence as I've gained top of page 1 Google organic ranking for this particular long tail keyword.

How do you find long tail keywords that people are searching for?

There are a number of paid for options but Google provide a very useful and free option. Go to www.google.co.uk and enter your chosen keyword (without clicking search or pressing enter). Google will then bring up a list of possible search options designed to save users time so they can just click from the options. Taking it a step further I then follow this process:

When on the search bar in Google start typing, 'Men's

watch a'. See what comes up; there may be nothing suitable for your business or nothing that you wish to rank for. In that case start going through the alphabet until you see something that is right for you, e.g.

'Men's watch b'
'Men's watch c'
'Men's watch d', and so on.

Complete the long tail keyword Google search and look at the quality of the results that come up. If the search results are dominated by top performing websites such as Amazon then it's unlikely you'll get quick results; this isn't to say it's a waste of time/effort but there may be quicker and easier keyword phrases to rank for.

You've chosen the long tail keyword(s) you want – how do you make them rank?

It's simple. Create better, more interesting content than what is already in position #1. I have achieved page 1 rankings for my clients using this strategy prior to gaining any backlinks (although having some good backlinks does help!).

If the content in position 1 is good, and it usually is, then you may need to be creative with how you outperform it. If their content is 1,500 words in length, making content that is 1,800 words in length may not cut it unless there is something very interesting or worthwhile in your content that explains the subject matter better. So what can you add to your content to make your page better and more relevant to achieve #1 ranking?

- Video – embed a YouTube/Vimeo video. It can either be you explaining what the written content is, adding more information or just explaining who you are and what makes you an authority on the subject.

- Infographic – As mentioned in another point in this book, infographics are very hot right now in the world of SEO and digital marketing. People have short attention spans – if you can summarise 1000 words of content in an eye catching image then users will tend to enjoy this.

- Interviews – this can sit alongside your content and either be written or in video format. Interviewing someone who can provide further insight into the topic can keep visitors on the page longer and help to see your page as more relevant than what is currently in position 1.

It seems quite easy – is it worth the effort?

Of course everyone would like to be position 1 of page 1 for the most competitive search terms in their industry. For whatever reason if this is not currently feasible then gaining long tail keyword ranking can have significant results. If your business or website was able to create content for one long tail keyword phrase a week, it could see your website have page 1 Google ranking for 40-50 search terms in a year.

Long tail keywords will of course have fewer searches than shorter keywords but I would always rather have 60-70% of a smaller percentage of traffic rather than 0-5% of traffic from a more competitive search term.

Lastly, by conducting long tail keyword work it can also have a really positive impact on starting to gain ranking for the shorter, more competitive keywords, so it's time to get to work!

1.5 Make your meta descriptions and page titles super appealing

Things do change but at the time of writing the length for page titles is 70 characters which includes spaces and punctuation and 260 characters for a meta description.

A website title and meta description informs users and search engines about what your website or particular webpage contains. I believe the majority of people don't put as much thought and effort into these as they potentially could. Conduct a search for just about anything and the majority of page titles and meta descriptions will generally follow a very similar theme, having targeted keywords placed and half decent copy. It's rare to find a meta description and title that stands out.

This is where I like to make my clients stand out from the crowd. I've seen some incredible results in click through rates simply by making meta descriptions more appealing and/or giving it a good call to action.

In some cases it simply isn't possible to get into position #1 of Google organic search results for some of the most competitive keywords; getting into positions 2-5, although challenging, can be far more achievable. The lion's share of clicks will still go to position 1, unless you look at standing out from the crowd, being innovative and giving search engine users a compelling reason to click on your link rather than the others. Adopting this method has helped many of my clients win significant amounts of traffic from being in positions 2-5 of search engine results.

As mentioned many, many times throughout this book, this can be a case of trial and error and it's worth testing a couple of pages first before rolling this out onto your site as a whole.

Here's an example of a generic page title and meta description from a company selling protein powders:

Protein ¦ Protein Supplements ¦ Sports Nutrition
Find all your protein products and bars from our store. Everything from protein powders through to shakes and bars to help build lean muscle.

Now there's nothing hugely wrong with this, other than a bit of keyword stuffing but it isn't very enticing. Imagine being a search engine user and seeing a meta description and title such as the one below by comparison which is promoting the same product:

STOP WHAT YOU ARE DOING RIGHT NOW! Protein Powder Mega Deal…
That's right, if you're looking for protein powder then you need to stop what you're doing and take advantage of this offer. Enter 'META' at checkout for an incredible 20% off!

If you were shopping for protein powder, which one do you think you would click?

I have tried this method with a wide range of clients spanning professional services through to ecommerce stores and seen some fantastic results. The nature of your sector and business will dictate just how creative and quirky you can get with your content and calls to action but I recommend creating engaging content that makes users act.

Keep an eye on Google Analytics to gauge the success of pages which you alter. While I recommend lots of testing, in this case it is worth keeping a pages title and meta description the same for a period of 3 months as it can take a few weeks for search engines to update with the latest content, and you will need to source meaningful statistics which you won't gain if you revise the content every 3-4 weeks.

1.6 Having a clear message

You can do all the advertising and marketing out there but if your business doesn't have a clear message then your business will underperform. There's a fantastic YouTube video with Simon Sinek during his Ted Talks presentation which I'd really recommend everyone in business watches. Simon Sinek looks at 'Starting With Why' – his theory is that customers don't buy what you do, they buy why you do it.

In my experience, very few businesses take the time out to clearly define why they are in business. By understanding why you are in business, it will allow you to create a clear message that can run across your marketing and advertising campaigns. I've come up with an example using a disabled lift, stairlift and home access client:

A 'standard' marketing message might be:

- Reliable stairlifts fitted by experienced engineers from a company trading over 25 years.

The above is a basic message but doesn't create any particular desire, unless you were desperately after a stairlift at that exact moment in time! A marketing message that is focused on 'why' can be far more powerful:

- Helping people lead an easier life in their home since 1995.

The marketing message doesn't look at the nuts and bolts of what the business does, rather what it does in a more holistic sense.

This is a particularly short section as the emphasis is now on you or your team to think about what message your business has and if it is fit for purpose. I'd very much recommend taking 20 minutes out of your day and watching the Simon Sinek video in full on YouTube.

1.7 Using Twitter for blogger outreach/gain backlinks

Twitter is an incredible tool allowing us to interact with bloggers and website owners around the world quickly and easily. Leveraging Twitter can save countless hours searching for and sending cold emails to bloggers who are looking to collaborate in exchange for a backlink.

Twitter allows you to quickly find influencers and authorities to make contact with as we're able to search hashtags that are relevant to our industry and see who is currently tweeting about it. Let's take men's fashion as an example; we could search for the following hashtags:

- #mensfashion
- #Mensstyle
- #Mensfashionblog
- #Mensfashionblogger etc.

The people posting with these type of hashtags will often be blog owners or perhaps an influencer.

How will you know if they really are an authority?

- Take a look at how many people follow them. I'd usually expect at least 3,000 as an absolute minimum.

- A lot of people are in the business of 'buying likes'

to artificially inflate how successful they are on social media. A good way to gauge if the account holders have genuine followers is to check what interactions are happening when he/she tweets. For example when someone with 20,000 followers tweets, you could normally expect a few dozen likes, maybe some retweets and replies depending on the type of update. If there are consistently no engagement on the account's posts, it's worth taking a minute to think why this might be.

- Click through to visit their website if they have one. Take a look at the quality of the design and content; you should start to get a feel very quickly for what makes the difference between a good website and an amateurish one.

- When visiting their website, take a look at some articles and see if they are currently backlinking or collaborating with anyone else.

How do I go about it?

To have any results it will require some time and effort on your part. Following someone on Twitter then immediately messaging them asking for a backlink is hardly ever going to work. Identify a handful of accounts that you would like to work with, then start interacting with them when they tweet; this can range from liking, retweeting or replying with your point of view/an answer or advice.

Taking this time and effort is really worthwhile as it makes you seem less of a stranger. I often get asked how long this process should continue for before making contact direct; while there's no perfect time period I try to take a common sense approach. If an account has around 3,000 followers, then spending 5-7 days consistently engaging with them could be enough to place you firmly on their radar. An account with 30,000+ followers will no doubt have many other people engaging with them so this can often require a good month or more in laying the foundations before getting in touch to see if you can work together.

What do you offer?

Don't go straight for the kill with a phrase like 'do you accept backlinks?'. Take a bit of time to visit their website, look at a specific article and provide them with some insight or a compliment. Let's go back to the men's fashion blog; if there's a piece of content relating to *how to choose the right tie* it can be worth messaging them and saying how interesting you found it and offer to contribute to the article further with any new insight you can provide.

Of course, this approach will need to be tweaked slightly depending on the industry you're going after but the logic will be the same across the board, offer to provide value!

Will it work?

It's a numbers game! I normally advise doing this approach with a handful of people and gauging the results; if no one replies, think about what you could have done differently, or what you could offer that might be more appealing.

Even if you've spent time doing the groundwork and have offered something really good, a lot of people simply won't reply as they're either too busy or are already inundated with requests, but don't give up; even if someone doesn't reply, keep them on your radar and engage with them consistently in a meaningful way.

1.8 Using Help a Reporter Out to gain quality backlinks

Gaining quality backlinks can be time consuming work that doesn't always yield results. Taking advantage of Help a Reporter Out (HARO) can be a quick way to show yourself as an industry expert and gain highly sought-after backlinks.

HARO is a resource that allows journalists who quickly need soundbites or opinions to get them from people with relevant sector experience.

How does it work?

- First you need to create an account on HARO, so head over to www.helpareporterout.com and sign up to start receiving daily HARO emails.

- When you have signed up you will start receiving emails everyday with a long list of journalists looking for input on a wide range of topics. The subjects will range from biotech through to lifestyle and fitness so there will be something for just about everyone.

- Read the emails each day to see if you can contribute and or answer a question that a journalist has. If you are able to offer something of value, you can send an email to the reporter.

- If your content is chosen for submission, then you can find yourself/your business on some of the most respected websites online very quickly.

What should you write?

- Most importantly, HARO isn't an opportunity for a sales pitch! Don't tell journalists about how great your products or services are, it simply won't be included in any editorials and you'll just be wasting your time.

- Keep it concise. The majority of journalists only want 2-3 sentences which can fit in well with their article. For busy people like us, this is fantastic! Gaining a backlink can often mean writing a guest post article containing thousands of words, this is your opportunity for a quality backlink with a fraction of the effort required.

- The journalists will state very clearly what they are looking for. Try not to deviate from this. If you can give a quick and clear answer or opinion to what they've requested your chances of success are far higher. (I know this sounds obvious but it's very easy to go off on a tangent, particularly if it's something you're passionate about).

- At the end of the article say who you are, what you do and briefly why you are an authority on the topic. Finally, and very importantly, include a link to your website/blog.

I have consistently gained quality backlinks for my clients over the past 5 years using HARO. Get signed up and start checking those emails, you have nothing to lose! The other great thing about HARO is that there are always a significant number of requests everyday, so you don't have to scan every email everyday religiously. If I'm very busy I may only check a HARO email once or twice a week but if I have some extra time to be proactive I'll be opening every one.

If you're not yet convinced, here are just some of the sites which use HARO:

- The New York Times
- TIME
- Reuters
- FOX News
- Mashable
- ABC
- And many, many, many more!

1.9 Taking part in podcasting

What's this got to do with my website, I can hear you ask. Read on.

Whatever business you're in, you will have a wealth of industry specific knowledge and opinions. Podcasting is becoming increasingly popular and in my opinion is only going to expand further. There are podcasts on just about every business and topic; it's generally perceived that those conducting or taking part in a podcast are an *expert* in their particular field, though of course this is not always the case.

Starting a podcast can be done very cheaply, it requires minimal equipment when doing a bootstrap start-up and hosting deals are very cheap with many free options. Whilst I do believe that starting your own podcast could be a significant long term boost for your business and personal brand, what it lacks in financial investment it makes up for in the investment of time required to build a popular podcast. For this reason we are looking to build relationships with other podcasters who already have an audience.

What are the benefits of being a guest on another podcast?

- You will build your network and meet influential people you probably wouldn't have done otherwise.

- You will automatically be placed in front of an audience without any of the legwork required to initially build up your own audience.

- You/your business will be perceived by many as being an expert/authority within the field.

- Gaining backlinks for your website from both the show notes as well as the podcast owner's website.

- If you do a good job in the episode it's likely you'll be interested (or even asked) to do more, meaning your exposure, networking and backlinks will continue to grow.

- You can embed the podcast episode onto your website which can build trust with new website visitors and portray you as an industry expert.

- It will provide you with some pretty powerful content to share across your social media channels which will again show you/your business as an authority in the sector.

- The majority of podcast interview recordings happen over Skype or similar software and can last anywhere from 10 minutes to an hour plus. The potential ROI for in many cases half an hour of your time can be significant and lasting (once the episode is out there, it can be heard at anytime from anyone around the world).

How do I get on a podcast?

First you need to decide which podcasts are right for you and your business; the way to do this is to head over to iTunes, search the relevant keywords and see what is available. There will most likely be a wide range of shows, ranging from the newly established through to the longstanding, well respected.

Before you make contact with anyone there's a few things you need to do:

- Think about what you're going to talk about/would like to talk about. What will you have to say that is of interest? Do you have a viewpoint? Do you have a strategy that works well? Most importantly, don't think you can go onto a podcast and plug your business, whether covertly or overtly; it just won't work, and if it does you run the risk of the episode not being published and blacklisting your name amongst other podcasters. Move away from the mindset of seeing it as an opportunity to advertise and more of an opportunity to inform your target audience about what you know, with useful information that can either be of interest or provide assistance.

- Listen to a few episodes of the podcast before you get in touch. This way when you do make contact you can provide the podcast host with some meaningful insight and have a better understanding of how your knowledge could fit into the show.

- Don't go straight in for the kill! The podcaster will probably never have heard of you before so a single, cold email or private message out of the blue asking to be on his/her show is unlikely to be successful. Perhaps leave them a 5* review on iTunes and inform them that you've done so to break the ice.

How do I find/make contact?

Currently I think the quickest and easiest way to make contact is through using social media, namely Twitter. Although this can vary depending on which social media channel the podcast owner is most active on. By listening to the podcast you'll hear the name of the hosts which you can search for on social media, follow and then make contact with.

Final thought

In my opinion, podcasting is going to continue to grow and grow. Those that embrace podcasting early are the ones who will yield the greatest results. Get yourself/your business on podcasts now and watch the opportunities as well as backlinks roll in over the coming weeks, months and years.

1.10 Embracing 'Live' features on social media channels

Facebook, Instagram LinkedIn and YouTube all allow individuals and business owners the opportunity to 'go live' on their platforms. It can seem daunting to press the record button and put yourself or your business out there to the world, but what are the potential opportunities if you do it well?

The primary reason for going live is that it will give your business an audience that it almost certainly wouldn't reach with a regular text or image-based post, unless you pay to promote it. At the time of writing, very few businesses are taking part in social media live recordings, meaning it is considerably less competitive than a regular text-based post. The social media channels therefore are far more likely to put those taking part in live in front of an audience.

How could I use 'live' in my business?

Going live can be done for a number of things but here are some of my favourites:

- A tour of your office, shop or business premises.

- Showing new products that have arrived.

- Day to day business operations. While many

business owners think this may seem mundane, customers can be very interested in what is happening.

- Showing how to find your business premises from well-known locations.

- Interviewing members of staff to allow potential customers to learn more about those who work in your business.

- Customer testimonials. A lot of customers can be real extroverts, asking them if they'd like to leave you a review on Facebook/Instagram/LinkedIn/ YouTube Live won't always work, but if you don't ask you don't get! A live customer testimonial can be seen as extremely authentic compared to rehearsed recordings and has the potential to skyrocket trust with potential customers.

- Your own vlog (video blog). If you're really passionate about your sector and have things to say about it, whether this is insight, advice or something else entirely, a vlog can be a great option to gain an audience.

These are just some of my favourite methods of going live on social media channels, there are many more things you can do but hopefully this will have given you a spark of inspiration. As you'll see from the above there's opportunities for both introverts and extroverts when 'going live'. If the thought of being on camera fills you with dread, then options such as tours of the office and recording new products will allow you to put your business on these channels without the need to get in front of the camera yourself.

How often should I go live?

Consistency is key, but if you have nothing to say or do, don't go on live just for the sake of it otherwise it will become dull for your audience. With my clients I look at the business and see what day fits best with going live. Initially if you could create a live video once a week and build it up to several times a week your exposure online should improve significantly as long as the content is good.

What are the benefits?

There are a few reasons why I love using live features:

- It's easy and quick! Compare going live to writing a 1000-word blog or researching and creating an infographic and you'll quickly realise that going live is considerably easier and less time intensive. You can have content marketing out to your audience requiring just a few minutes of your time.

- You'll reach a wider audience. As already mentioned, more people will start to see your business. This is important, the majority won't buy from someone they've never heard of before – by going live you'll take an audience of potential customers into the awareness stage of your business.

- Businesses using live across social media platforms are widely seen as innovative and forward thinking.

- Almost certainly your competitors won't be doing this currently, or if they are, only a fraction of them will be doing so. By embracing live on social media you'll be getting in front of an audience on a platform that the vast majority of your competitors won't be.

All that remains now is to plan what your first live broadcast will be! Get your smartphone ready, make sure you're looking smart and put yourself out there to the world. Good luck and enjoy!

1.11 Infographics

Content marketing is important. Many people assume content marketing only relates to creating written articles. Embracing infographics can offer your business serious exposure as well as some quality backlinks if your infographic provides useful information.

If you're not sure what an infographic is do a quick search online and come back to me! An infographic is a visual aid which allows content creators to get across a great deal of information in a quick and eye-pleasing way. Rather than writing hundreds of words of content and quoting dry statistics, an infographic helps to bring content to life, make it look appealing and can have a high engagement rate.

How do you make an infographic?

You have a few options depending on how much time you have available, your budget and whether or not you have an eye for design. The three options:

- Get someone else to do it! My personal favourite. If you're not a designer don't 'have a go' or spend countless hours trying to get good at it when there are websites such as fiverr.com and peopleperhour.com that have designers from around the world ready to create such designs starting from around £15.

- If you're just starting out or you don't have much of a budget there are some free infographic templates out there which will allow you to create your own infographics. The only downside is that templates can be quite restrictive.

- If you have a lot of time on your hands and have a flair for design it's time to invest in Photoshop and purchase a course on Udemy or start watching some YouTube videos.

How will your infographic get backlinks?

Many people worry that other site owners will simply save their infographic image, use it on their website and not attribute it with a backlink. While this can still happen, the savvy infographic creator will offer website owners a simple copy and paste embed code which will automatically generate a 'do follow' backlink to your website.

Siege Media have a free option that can quickly turn your infographic into an embed code, take a look for yourself:

https://www.siegemedia.com/embed-code-generator

Wherever you place your infographic, whether on your website or social media, post the embed code with it/underneath it so people can quickly and easily use your content.

The second way to gain high quality backlinks is both my favourite and the most time consuming. What it takes in time is well worth it when the results come in. Firstly, find who are performing best in your space (I do this by seeing who are in the top positions on Google for your chosen keywords) and then find out where their backlinks are coming from. I like to do this using either moz.com or ahrefs.com, although there are some free versions available but I find these to be the most reliable; if they're new to you there are some free trials available. Enter the url of your competitors and you will see who is linking to them and what content they are linking to. If they are linking to a blog article or some interesting information, turn this content into an infographic! (Be sure you cite your sources in the infographic – make sure you don't forget to do this).

Then comes the time consuming part, reaching out to everyone who has linked to your competitors' content. It's time consuming but it's quite an easy win compared to traditional link building strategies as you will know that the site owner is already interested in the content, you have just repurposed it in a visually appealing, more digestible way. Make it even easier for them by including the embed code at the end of your email to them so it's super quick and easy for them to update the site.

My favourite ways to reach out to website owners:

- Follow them on Twitter, spend a few days liking their posts and maybe even do a few retweets.

Follow this up with a direct message saying how you'd like to help them with your new and improved version of the content they're currently linking to.

- Do some research to find out who the website owners are and add them on LinkedIn (more on this later!) then follow the same process as Twitter.

- This has never been very successful for me when compared to the other two strategies but completing the websites contact forms and/or sending an email to the site can also work.

Part 2:

Convert More Traffic

2.1 Using video to engage website visitors

Research has shown that embedding a video on your website can help to significantly decrease bounce rate and increase user engagement.

When I mention making a video to most people, I can actually see the blood drain from their face at the thought of having to be in front of the camera. When you start to think about the expense of bringing in a good cameraman and editor it has the potential to be quite an expensive trial, so what's the solution?

Whiteboard and/or cartoon animation videos!

There are some incredible video animators from all around the world on sites such as PeoplePerHour.com who offer great videos along with a professional voiceover for between £40 - £150+. If you've no idea what a whiteboard animation video is, go take a look on peopleperhour.com and watch a few examples. For very short animations I've recently started using biteable.com which for a low monthly fee of around £30 allows users to quickly and easily create videos with no experience required.

What should a video contain?

Attention spans are short! So if your homepage or service pages are very text heavy then it's likely a high percentage will be opting to click away instead of sifting through all the content. Your video could last anywhere from 30 seconds up to 2 minutes to quickly get across who you are, what your business does and the reasons to use you. Here are some other ideas to get more website visitors turning into engaged users who become enquiries, leads and sales:

- Quickly explain a problem that someone could be facing then how your product or service could solve that problem.

- Engage your website visitor by providing them with some useful knowledge about your product or service.

- A great call to action! Whatever it is you want your website visitors to do, whether it's get in touch for a free consultation or make a purchase, create a clear call to action in your video and if possible provide an incentive if they do take action.

What else can a video be good for?

You've invested around £50 in a good video that quickly gets across who you are, what you do and how you do it. First things first, upload the video onto YouTube and get it embedded on your website.

After you've done this it's time to start getting your video on as many different platforms as possible:

- Vimeo – similar to YouTube, just not as popular but still a very good source of potential traffic.

- Upload the video to Facebook (this isn't just sharing the YouTube link, actually upload the video to your Facebook page along with a title and description).

- DailyMotion.

- Flickr.

- The list goes on but these are some great options to get you started.

Having a video can be a great piece of content to share across your social media platforms. This piece of content really will be the gift that keeps on giving. I have clients who have had videos created 5-6 years ago that are still getting tens of thousands of views a year resulting in leads and enquiries and it costs them nothing!

2.2 Reducing your website's bounce rate

Getting traffic to your website will either cost you time or money. Whether you're running pay per click campaigns, offline paid advertising, paying a marketing agency for SEO services or putting your valuable time into learning and implementing SEO, it's an investment.

A bounce rate is calculated as the number of people who land on a page of your website and then leave before looking at any other pages. As an example, if 10 people land on your website and all leave after looking at just one page, your bounce rate would be 100%. If 10 people land on your website, 5 leave immediately whilst the other five engage with it further by reading blogs, About pages or other content then your bounce rate would be 50%.

If you're investing time and money into driving traffic to your website through whatever means, then having a high bounce rate will result in a high percentage of that money effectively being wasted.

A high bounce rate has a number of negative impacts, but I believe the two most important ones are:

- It can show Google that your website content isn't engaging as people leave immediately, this can see your website drop in search rankings.

- Potential customers aren't engaging with your website and are far less likely to become a customer.

If you don't know what your bounce rate is, check (or install) Google Analytics. As always, keep checking and testing as your bounce rate might be in a good position and then start creeping up over weeks and months. I see bounce rate analytics as one of the most important facets of the information available in Google Analytics.

There isn't a set guide but here's what I think about bounce rate percentages:

0-20% - Your website is amongst the best around!
21-40% - You have a very engaging website.
41-50% - Better than average (in my opinion).
51-60% - Good but room for improvement.
61-100% - Start planning and testing some changes!

How can you reduce your bounce rate?

- Site speed optimisation – if your website loads slowly then it will perform poorly. Run a free check on Google Site Speed Insights; if your site speed is running at amber or red then you need to make real improvements to reduce your bounce rate and improve the user experience. Site speed optimisation has the potential to be technical so if you're not confident with this I'd recommend outsourcing the task to a coder using People Per

Hour or Fiverr.

- Place a video on website pages that have a high bounce rate. Research has shown simply adding a video to a webpage can have a significant impact on bounce rate and user engagement.

- Does your content look boring? Even if your content is great, if a visitor lands on a page full of text then it can often be seen as too much effort. Break content up with imagery, header tags, infographics and video to make your page more visually appealing.

- Do you have annoying pop ups? Having annoying pop ups for email subscriptions and other deals can have visitors quickly clicking the X button.

- Make your website 'sticky' – I like the phrase sticky, it simply means keeping your visitors on the site for longer. This can be done by creating appealing links within the content to take visitors to another page. Don't do this to just artificially reduce your bounce rate, actually provide fantastic content that will provide a great user experience. As an example, if a blog article with a high bounce rate was called 'Ways to make more money from home', having a clickable link to an engaging article that is linked or follows on from this content can prove very effective, e.g. 'Learn our top 3 ways to start making money from home right now'.

- Make sure your website is mobile friendly – Just about every website is these days but it's always worth checking if you're not sure. If a particular page(s) has a high bounce rate, visit those pages from various devices to ensure there are no issues.

- Provide an enticing call to action that makes visitors want to get in touch. We'll cover this in a different section but if you can provide a compelling call to action it's both a fantastic user experience and it will also drive down your bounce rate. Whether you offer a free ebook, resources, a consultation or something else, think about what your visitors may be after.

- Ask people what they think of your website. Don't ask friends or family as they'll almost always not give you the constructive criticism you're looking for and potentially need. Whether you go to forums, Facebook pages or go outside of your regular network for insight, take the time to understand what people do and don't like about your website and then fix the issues.

Remember that making changes to your website won't have an automatic impact on your bounce rate. When making changes be sure to give at least 4-6 weeks to see what impact the changes have made on your website. It's particularly useful to drive down the individual webpages that have the highest bounce rates; I've seen many cases where a business would have a respectable bounce rate but 5-10 pages are bringing in a lot of traffic with a bounce rate that is through the roof, creating a high bounce rate overall.

If individual webpages are already working with a low bounce rate then leave those pages alone as making changes might have a negative impact if they're currently doing very well. Focus on making changes to the pages which are struggling.

Many people forget about or don't value bounce rate work, but think about how much easier it is to work at converting traffic you're already getting anyway as opposed to going out there and trying to win even more traffic at your current bounce rate.

2.3 Having a great 'About Us' page to increase enquiries

Your website's 'About' page is a real opportunity and one that many business owners fail to take advantage of.

Having worked with countless websites across a wide range of sectors over the past 10 years I've spent a lot of time looking at Google Analytics accounts. One thing that always stands out to me is how often and how much time website visitors spend on the About pages of a website before getting in touch, or exiting a site.

I believe that most people looking at an About page are almost sold on your product or service and want to get a bit of extra reassurance before getting in touch or going through the checkout. Remember that website visitors most likely won't know or have heard of you or your business before, so you need to build trust with them to show that you're a real business.

Here's what I've found to be the best ingredients for a successful About Us page:

- Pictures of company owners and staff members. Most people shudder at the thought of having their headshot online but it really works. *People buy from people,* by putting images of your team online it takes away any notion that you're just another faceless website.

- Bios/descriptions of staff. This always works very well in my experience. Along with the photograph giving a snapshot of information about each member of staff, this can range from professional to quirky depending on the nature of your business.

- Photographs of your office, retail store, premises. Again, building trust! Show your website visitors that you're a real business.

- Customer testimonials: It's that word again, trust! If possible try to get a video testimonial from customers to embed on your website. This doesn't have to be an expensive film crew, it's fine to use your smart phone; what it lacks in professional quality it will make up for in authenticity.

These are what I have found to be the most successful ingredients in a successful About Us page, however every business is different. Consistently log in to Google Analytics and see how many people are landing on your About page and how long they're spending on it. If you notice that the time spent on the page is less than 10 seconds, or the page has a huge exit rate, then it is not doing it's job properly. It will then be up to you to make refinements to make the page more engaging; this can range from minor tweaks such as altering the page order, increasing the font size used or adding more relevant imagery and or videos to improve engagement.

Remember, human psychology is not an exact art! Google Analytics will provide you with a wealth of information about how users interact with every page of your site, use this information and make adjustments to ensure your website is as strong as it can possibly be.

2.4 Using virtual chat to increase conversions (Tawk)

We're running businesses in an age when people want almost instantaneous answers and information. If your website doesn't offer visitors a quick and easy way to communicate then it's likely you'll be having missed opportunities. Using instant live chat can offer your business a simple way for visitors to communicate which requires extremely little effort on their part. I've used the Tawk plugin on a range of websites from ecommerce right through to technical service-based businesses and it has proven to be a very useful addition each time.

If your website is getting visitors, those who may become customers will almost certainly have questions; they might range from how much your services cost, how much shipping costs are to certain countries, through to technical questions relating to your product or service. I have seen significant uplifts in conversions by businesses engaging with live chat platforms and 'talking' to visitors, many of which then proceed through the checkout or get in touch to find out more now that their questions have been addressed.

What does embracing live chat portray to potential customers about your business?

- Firstly, it highlights that you're a real, legitimate business.

- It will be assumed by most that you will have staff taking care of live chat so the business should be of a fairly big size rather than a one man band.

- Your business takes customer service seriously.

- Your company will almost certainly be innovative or advanced to embrace such technology whilst the majority do not.

There are many different platforms out there and I wouldn't like to recommend any in particular. I can only say that I've used Tawk and been very happy with it, but this is not an endorsement! Do your own research to make sure you choose a platform which is right for you and your website.

Won't someone (probably me!) need to be locked to my computer 24/7 in case someone gets in touch?

Not at all! My clients have set up designated times for the chat software to be marked as online. If they're at their desk then it's no problem sending replies; what I've really liked is the ability to download the Tawk app and receive notifications just as you would with a text or a phone call, informing you that a website visitor has sent a message.

If you see this as a drain on your time it might be worth looking at hiring a virtual assistant company who are able to communicate with website visitors if you have the budget in place.

As mentioned again and again, trial the technology if you think it could be right for you and keep on testing. Analyse Google Analytics to see if website visitors stay on your site longer/visit more pages. How many potential customers get in touch using this platform compared to when you didn't have it, and ultimately does it result in an uplift of sales.

2.5 Exit intent software

When focusing on a digital marketing strategy I have found that a lot of people don't pay much attention to the traffic that their website is already receiving.

In some cases we have had better results focusing on conversion optimisation techniques to get leads from current levels of traffic rather than focusing on going after even more visitors. One of the ways in which we have had some very good success is with exit intent software. There are a number of free and paid for versions out there depending on which content management system you use and it can be a great tool to increase leads if your call to action is appealing.

Exit intent software serves as a pop up which is displayed to people who are getting ready to exit your site (moving their cursor over the X to close the page). Some examples of good exit intent messages which have worked well for our clients:

- Can't find something you're looking for? Give us a call on ……….

- DON'T LEAVE US! Enter 'PROMO' at checkout for £10 off your order today!

- Ready to leave? Why not contact us to claim a free initial consultation

Your call to action will depend upon the business you're in. Remember that human psychology is not an exact science so if your exit intent isn't getting any results it may not be the software at fault, your call to action may not be appealing enough to make visitors act. If you're not seeing results it's time to change your call to action until you get one that works.

Remember that exit intent software will show to people who are just about to leave your site, so the success rate will be very low; however even with a success rate of just 0.5% this can add up to a significant number of leads over a 12 month period. Turning even a fraction of website leavers into leads and customers is well worth testing this software, particularly when there are free plugins available online.

2.6 Landing pages

Bringing traffic to your website will either cost you time or money, simple as that. Most people I meet are very focused on bringing more and more traffic to their website and pay little regard for the traffic they are already receiving. I have seen the implementation of strong landing pages have a significant impact on website engagement and conversions.

What is a landing page?

As the name suggests it is a page of your website that a visitor would 'land' on. For best results landing pages are usually implemented on pay per click and social media campaigns. I'll take a law firm as an example. They are running a pay per click campaign on 'reasons to have a law firm write a will'.

Scenario One: Visitors clicking their PPC advertisement are taken to either the website homepage or the general service page. You'll be sick of hearing this from me but it's important so I'll be saying it a lot – people when they go online are lazy, very lazy! If they click an advert, they will want to land on a perfect page that provides them with more information on exactly what they have just clicked. If they click and land on a website homepage it's usually faster to hit the back button and go to the next position down to find what they're after rather than navigate their way through a website.

Scenario Two: The law firm run an extremely niche and tight pay per click campaign; for example, let's say they're running a PPC campaign promoting their will writing services to police officers. When the person clicks the campaign they would be taken to a landing page which gets across the firm's expertise, shows past experience and has a theme in line with their target audience, e.g. it may have some copyright free images of police officers on there. If the person clicking the advert is a police officer thinking about writing a will, then this 'landing page' should be considerably more appealing and make far more people get in touch rather than landing on a general service page or homepage.

What should a landing page look like?

I can't get this across with words alone so please take a minute to go to Google and run a search for 'great landing page examples'. There are various formats that landing pages can take but you'll get a good idea of how some of the leading experts are using landing page layouts to maximise results.

What should a landing page contain?

- Firstly, a great design that is appealing. If you're not a designer, source one on sites such as Peopleperhour.com or fiverr.com – prices can start from around £10 and the return on investment should be significant if you get your message right.

- Specific testimonials that show your expertise and customer satisfaction. If possible, video testimonials can work incredibly well.

- A clear call to action that shows visitors exactly what to do if they want to get in touch. Most importantly, don't give too many options. If your landing page has numerous differing options such as signing up for email marketing, claiming a free consultation, completing a contact form etc, then it's going to be less effective. Decide one thing that you want the visitors to do, then only give that option. Whether you want them to sign up to receive your email newsletter or be a straightforward lead through the contact form, then focus on that one thing.

- Display any logos that can act as social proof. This can range from being members of a Chamber of Commerce, trade association or the logos of some reputable clients that you have or are currently working with.

How many landing pages should I have?

This is up to you. I have seen websites with dozens of landing pages. I worked with a cleaning company a few years ago that specialised in office cleans and they had landing pages for solicitors, accountants, government contracts, design agencies, the list truly went on and on! It worked for them so they were happy. If you are brand new to creating landing pages for your website then I would recommend focusing on one or two until you see results and can then scale up.

How will I get people to my landing page?

Landing pages aren't usually ranked highly by Google as they're short on content and to the point, so you'll be looking to run pay per click advertising campaigns to bring traffic to your landing page. At this moment in time I would recommend spreading your PPC budget between Google Ads and Facebook.

How will I make my landing page convert?

TEST, TEST, TEST! Most likely you won't get a perfect landing page on your first attempt so keep a close eye on your advertising spend and use Google Analytics to see how visitors are engaging with your landing page and how many visitors are converting. Keep making tweaks to your page until you're happy with the conversion rate and then you can creep the budget up higher and higher when the formula is correct.

2.7 Creating an engaging 404 error page

If you're not sure what a 404 error page is, take a minute and do a Google Images search to see some examples.

404 error pages are what the name suggests, they're pages that have an error meaning they're broken or no longer exist. This can potentially be a huge issue as the bounce rate on 404 error pages are understandably through the roof as they're usually quite ugly pages that display a warning and give a really poor impression of the website in question.

Many people don't take the time and effort (mainly as most don't know) to go about designing an innovative and interesting 404 error page that is far more likely to keep visitors on the site when compared to the generic error page.

How you go about designing your page will depend on what sector you're in but a great 404 page will keep visitors entertained; one of the best examples I've seen is the use of an autoplay video which explained what the company did and gave a very obvious and clear link back to the site's homepage.

There are lots of different ways your 404 error page can be set out, ranging from quirky to professional. Again it's a good idea to go to Google Images and run a search for 'Great 404 error page' to see how some of the best marketeers out there are doing it and give you inspiration for what to do with yours.

How do I get a 404 error page designed?

If you're not a designer yourself, the quickest and simplest option is to outsource it. Using freelancer websites such as People Per Hour will put you in front of thousands of potential designers who will create a design to your specifications for a minimal fee. When the design is complete it will then need to be coded into a webpage; again, if this isn't your thing, place the task on a freelancer website and find the right person to do it for you.

How do I remove 404 errors?

The longer your website is around and the more changes that are made to it, the more likely 404 errors are likely to occur. One of my favourite tools to discover 404 errors on a website is the Moz Crawl report. If you don't have a Moz subscription it can also be done through Google Search Console by clicking on 'crawl errors' under 'diagnostics' and then clicking 'not found'. You may be surprised how many 404 errors are there; it is then the tedious job of fixing the pages or setting up 301 redirects using a WordPress plugin such as the Eggplant 301 redirect. Hopefully this will be as technical as this book gets. If this paragraph makes absolutely no sense to you, get onto YouTube and watch an explainer video of this being done.

2.8 LinkedIn marketing tactics to show you and your business as the expert

LinkedIn can be a crowded space with many business owners and professionals all looking to sell and promote themselves and their services. How will you get exposure and win some business on this platform?

First thing to note is that LinkedIn marketing won't yield a quick win. Whatever product or service you're planning to promote on LinkedIn there will already be people on the platform doing exactly that. It is going to take time to build a network and get them to *know, like and trust* you. This is only to be expected though, you wouldn't plan to walk into the office of your ideal customer out of the blue and expect them to buy from you immediately, so why would they do it online?

Step One – Building a Network

This is where a lot of people go wrong. Don't just add anyone and everyone so you have an overly inflated number of connections. What use are 5000 connections that yield no business? Decide who your ideal customer is and start connecting with those people, for example it might be accountants in Manchester.

Step Two – Don't Be Tempted To Sell

It's tempting to send a message over to a new connection

immediately telling them all about yourself, what you do and how you can help them; now truly isn't the time! The success rate will be microscopic and you'll be far more likely to annoy your ideal target customer.

Step Three – Add Value

Whatever your business is, you'll know your stuff. You'll have interesting stories, tips, advice, information and insight on current trends within your sector. If you consistently provide interesting, relevant and useful content for your target audience you will be recognised.

Step Four – Make People Like You

When you have made some connections it's time to actually connect with them. When they are posting updates, asking for advice/tips, or knowing LinkedIn they're just showing off, use this as an opportunity to either 'like' their update or put a meaningful comment under their post. By doing this consistently (be careful not to go overboard so you don't look like a stalker!) your name will start to get on their radar and when you do come around to sending them a direct message further down the line it's no longer a 'cold' sell.

Step Five – Create Content That Brings LinkedIn Users To Your Website

This is my favourite LinkedIn tactic. Write a great piece of content and place it on your website as a blog.

When this is done, replicate the first paragraph and half of the first sentence of the second paragraph, and publish this as a LinkedIn article; following this, use the text 'READ MORE...' and make this a clickable link to take readers to your website to read the rest of the content.

Step Six – Be Seen As A Person Of Authority In Your Industry

This can be a really quick and easy win. You will know your industry, start following industry blogs and news websites; when something interesting or noteworthy is reported, post it on LinkedIn and say what you think about it. It may be good news, bad news, have a certain impact on service users, etc. Even though you are not the author, by voicing an educated opinion on trending matters in your industry you can come to be seen as an expert with very little effort.

2.9 Internal linking for quick success and making your website sticky

An internal link is a clickable piece of text or an image which takes the website user to another page of your website. An example would be 'Click here to visit our Contact page', the words 'click here' would contain a link to the Contact page meaning users can quickly and easily navigate your website.

The first advantage for business owners and digital marketers is to make it easy for website users to navigate their website, keep them on the site for longer, and have them view more pages than they likely would have done if the internal links weren't there. These three simple things will almost certainly reduce the bounce rate of your website and increase the time spent on your site both of which are widely believed to be ranking factors from Google. In addition to this, generally the longer someone spends time engaging with your site the more likely they are to become a customer, lead or return visitor.

What pages should I link to?

This will depend on your website. If you run an ecommerce store with hundreds of products and dozens of pages there may be a significant amount of internal links to be built. If you run an accountancy practice with a handful of pages, then it will be much quicker and easier. Here are the pages I usually link to:

- Contact page.

- About Us page (only if the About Us page is strong and contains useful/interesting information).

- Service/product pages (this can be done very effectively when writing blog articles, when mentioning a product or service; make the text clickable and link to the page you're referring to).

- From blog to blog – the bounce rate on blogs can be very high on many websites, with visitors landing on a blog article after a Google search, reading the content, getting what they needed and then leaving the site. By creating appealing internal links you're far more likely to keep the blog traffic on the site for longer; a great way of doing this is towards the end of the article think about what else this reader might be interested in and then provide an option to click to read more about it in the form of another blog article or page of your website. I'll take a fitness blog as an example: a blog article relating to 'Best supplements for distance runners' is of course aimed at distance runners and will be read by people who are interested in this; towards the end of the article place an enticing internal link such as 'Click here to read our latest blog on the 5 things you need to be doing if you want to improve as a distance runner'. This has worked incredibly well for me time and time again with a wide range of clients and I'd very much recommend doing it with your blog.

It's important to remember that internal linking is firstly done to help your website visitors quickly and easily find what they're looking for. Don't be tempted to go overboard and fill your content with internal links; while it will be different depending on the sector, I normally aim to have 1-2 internal links per 500 words of content.

www.ingramcontent.com/pod-product-compliance
Lightning Source LLC
Chambersburg PA
CBHW071029050326
40689CB00014B/3579